PIANO • VOCAL • GUITAR

ULTIMATE

CHRISTMAS

• 100 SEASONAL FAVORITES •

ISBN 0-88188-158-9

HAL•LEONARD® CORPORATION

7777 W. BLUEMOUND RD. P.O. BOX 13819 MILWAUKEE, WI 53213

Visit Hal Leonard Online at
www.halleonard.com

ULTIMATE CHRISTMAS

PIANO•VOCAL•GUITAR

• 100 SEASONAL FAVORITES •

A CAROLING WE GO

Music and Lyrics by
JOHNNY MARKS

AWAY IN A MANGER

Traditional
Words by JOHN T. McFARLAND (v.3)
Music by JAMES R. MURRAY

A -

way   in a   man - ger,   no   crib   for   a

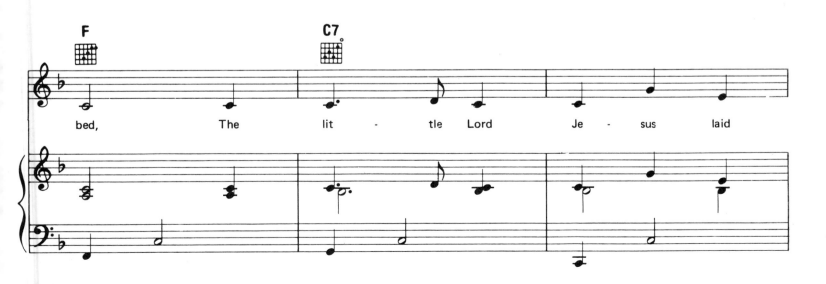

bed,   The   lit - tle   Lord   Je - sus   laid

ALMOST DAY

Words and Music by
HUDDIE LEDBETTER

Chick-ens a-crowin' for mid-night, It's Al-most Day;

Chick-ens a-crowin' for mid-night, It's Al-most Day.

Can-dy canes___ and sug-ar plums,___ On Christ-mas day;

ANGELS FROM THE REALMS OF GLORY

Words by JAMES MONTGOMERY
Music by HENRY T. SMART

ANGELS WE HAVE HEARD ON HIGH

Traditional French Carol
Translated by JAMES CHADWICK

Shep - herds, why this ju - bi - lee?

Why your joy - ous strains pro - long?

What the glad - some tid - ings be

Which in - spire your heaven - ly song? Glo -

AULD LANG SYNE

Words by ROBERT BURNS
Traditional Scottish Melody

AWAY IN A MANGER

Anonymous Text (vv.1,2)
Text by JOHN T. McFARLAND (v.3)
Music by JONATHAN E. SPILLMAN

BRING A TORCH, JEANNETTE, ISABELLA

17th Century French Provençal Carol

Hasten now, good folk of the village,
Hasten now, the Christ Child to see.
You will find him asleep in a manger,
Quietly come and whisper softly,
Hush, hush, Peacefully now He slumbers,
Hush, hush, Peacefully now He sleeps.

CAROL OF THE BELLS

Ukrainian Christmas Carol

Exuberantly

CAROLING, CAROLING

Words by WIHLA HUTSON
Music by ALFRED BURT

THE CHIPMUNK SONG

Words and Music by
ROSS BAGDASARIAN

Christ - mas, hur - ry fast! Want a plane that loops the loop; Me, I want a hu - la hoop. We can hard - ly stand the wait, Please Christ - mas don't be late.

CHRIST WAS BORN ON CHRISTMAS DAY

Traditional

C-H-R-I-S-T-M-A-S

Words by JENNY LOU CARSON
Music by EDDY ARNOLD

Moderato (with expression)

CHRISTMAS TIME IS HERE

Words by LEE MENDELSON
Music by VINCE GUARALDI

COVENTRY CAROL

Words by ROBERT CROO
Traditional English Melody

3. Herod the king,
   In his raging,
   Charged he hath this day.
   His men of might,
   In his own sight,
   All young children to slay.

4. That woe is me,
   Poor child for thee!
   And ever morn and day,
   For thy parting
   Neither say nor sing
   By by, lully lullay!

THE CHRISTMAS WALTZ

Words by SAMMY CAHN
Music by JULE STYNE

39

DANCE OF THE SUGAR PLUM FAIRY
from THE NUTCRACKER

By PYOTR IL'YICH TCHAIKOVSKY

DO YOU HEAR WHAT I HEAR

Words and Music by NOEL REGNEY
and GLORIA SHAYNE

DECK THE HALL

Traditional Welsh Carol

THE FIRST NOEL

17th Century English Carol
Music from *W. Sandys' Christmas Carols*

Additional Lyrics

2. They looked up and saw a star
   Shining in the East, beyond them far.
   And to the earth it gave great light
   And so it continued both day and night.
   Refrain

3. And by the light of that same star,
   Three wise men came from country far;
   To seek for a King was their intent,
   And to follow the star wherever it went.
   Refrain

4. This star drew nigh to the northwest,
   O'er Bethlehem it took its rest;
   And there it did both stop and stay,
   Right over the place where Jesus lay.
   Refrain

5. Then entered in those wise men three,
   Full reverently upon their knee;
   And offered there in His presence,
   Their gold, and myrrh, and frankincense.
   Refrain

THE FRIENDLY BEASTS

Traditional English Carol

beasts a - round Him stood,

Je - sus our broth - er, kind and good.

Additional Lyrics

2. "I," said the donkey, shaggy and brown,
   "I carried His mother up hill and down;
   I carried her safely to Bethlehem town."
   "I," said the donkey, shaggy and brown.

3. "I," said the cow all white and red,
   "I gave Him my manger for His bed;
   I gave Him my hay to pillow His head."
   "I," said the cow all white and red.

4. "I," said the sheep with curly horn,
   "I gave Him my wool for His blanket warm;
   He wore my coat on Christmas morn."
   "I," said the sheep with curly horn.

5. "I," said the dove from the rafters high,
   "I cooed Him to sleep so He would not cry;
   We cooed Him to sleep, my mate and I."
   "I," said the dove from the rafters high.

6. Thus every beast by some good spell,
   In the stable dark was glad to tell
   Of the gift he gave Emanuel,
   The gift he gave Emanuel.

FROSTY THE SNOW MAN

Words and Music by STEVE NELSON
and JACK ROLLINS

FUM, FUM, FUM

Traditional Catalonian Carol

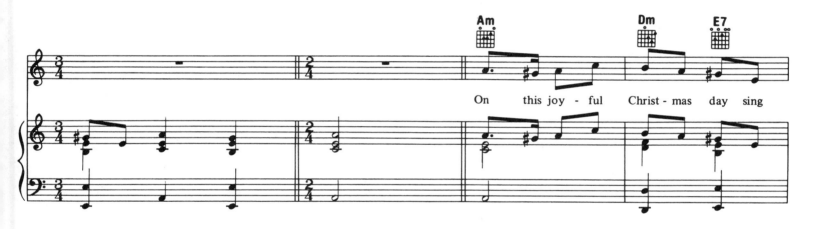

Fum. Thanks to God for hol - i - days, sing Fum, Fum,

Fum. Now we___ all our voic - es raise, and sing a song of grate - ful

praise,_____ Cel - e - brate in song and stor - y, all the

won - ders of his glo - ry, Fum, Fum, Fum.

GESU BAMBINO

Text by FREDERICK H. MARTENS
Music by PIETRO YON

Lyrics (first system, vocal entry): When / Nel

E | B7/E | E | B7/E | E | A/E | B7/E | E

blos - soms flow - ered 'mid__ the snows   Up - on   a   win - ter night_____   Was
l'u - mi - le__ ca - pan - na   Nel   fred - doe po - ver - tá,_____   È

E | B7/E | E | B/E | E | A/E | E

born__ the Child,__ the Christ - mas Rose,__ the   King__ of Love__ and Light._____   The
na - to il san - to par - go - lo   Che il   mon - do a - do - re - rà._____   O

GOOD CHRISTIAN MEN, REJOICE

14th Century Latin Text
Translated by JOHN MASON NEALE
14th Century German Melody

Good Chris-tian Men, Re - joice____ with heart and soul and voice,____ Give ye heed to
Good Chris-tian Men, Re - joice____ with heart and soul and voice,____ Now ye hear of

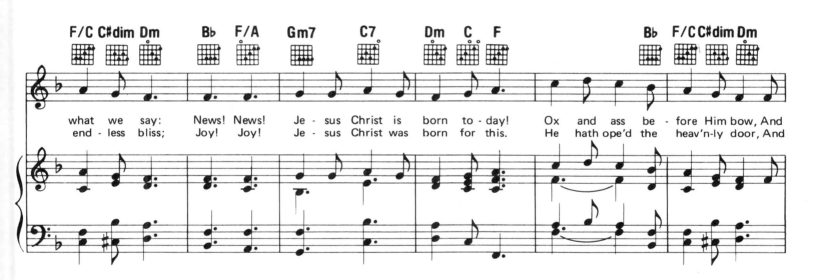

what we say: News! News! Je - sus Christ is born to - day! Ox and ass be - fore Him bow, And
end - less bliss; Joy! Joy! Je - sus Christ was born for this. He hath ope'd the heav'n-ly door, And

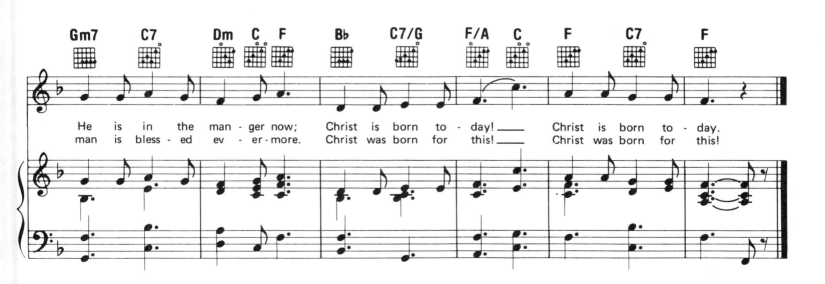

He is in the man-ger now; Christ is born to - day!____ Christ is born to - day.
man is bless - ed ev - er-more. Christ was born for this!____ Christ was born for this!

GO, TELL IT ON THE MOUNTAIN

African-American Spiritual
Verses by JOHN W. WORK, JR.

Fine

moun - tain, That Je - sus Christ _ is born.

When I was a seek - er, I sought both night and
He made me a watch - man up - on the cit - y

day; I asked the Lord to help me, And
wall; And if I am a Christ - ian, I

He showed me the way. _____
am the least of all. _____

D.S. al Fine

GOD REST YE MERRY, GENTLEMEN

19th Century English Carol

God rest ye mer - ry, gen - tle - men, Let
Beth - le - hem, in Jew - ry This

noth - ing you dis - may, For Je - sus Christ our
bless - ed you babe was born, And laid with - in a

Sav - ior was born up - on this day, To
man - ger, Up - on this bless - ed morn; To

65

GOOD KING WENCESLAS

Words by JOHN M. NEALE
Music from *Piae Cantiones*

2.
"Hither page, and stand by me,
  If thou know'st it, telling,
Yonder peasant, who is he?
  Where and what his dwelling?"
"Sire, he lives a good league hence,
  Underneath the mountain;
Right against the forest fence,
  By Saint Agnes' fountain."

3.
"Bring me flesh, and bring me wine,
  Bring me pine-logs hither;
Thou and I will see him dine,
  When we bear them thither."
Page and monarch forth they went,
  Forth they went together;
Through the rude winds wild lament:
  And the bitter weather.

4.
"Sire, the night is darker now,
  And the wind blows stronger;
Fails my heart, I know not how,
  I can go not longer."
"Mark my footsteps, my good page,
  Tread thou in them boldly:
Thou shalt find the winter's rage
  Freeze thy blood less coldly."

5.
In his master's steps he trod,
  Where the snow lay dinted;
Heat was in the very sod
  Which the saint had printed.
Therefore, Christain men, be sure,
  Wealth or rank possessing,
Ye who now will bless the poor,
  Shall yourselves find blessing.

THE GREATEST GIFT OF ALL

Words and Music by
JOHN JARVIS

HAPPY HOLIDAY

from the Motion Picture Irving Berlin's HOLIDAY INN

Words and Music by
IRVING BERLIN

HAPPY XMAS
(War Is Over)

Words and Music by JOHN LENNON
and YOKO ONO

78

HARK! THE HERALD ANGELS SING

Words by CHARLES WESLEY
Altered by GEORGE WHITEFIELD
Music by FELIX MENDELSSOHN-BARTHOLDY
Arranged by WILLIAM H. CUMMINGS

HERE WE COME A-WASSAILING

Traditional

3. We have got a little purse
   Of stretching leather skin;
   We want a little money
   To line it well within:

4. God bless the master of this house,
   Likewise the mistress too;
   And all the little children
   That round the table go:

THE HOLLY AND THE IVY

18th Century English Carol

85

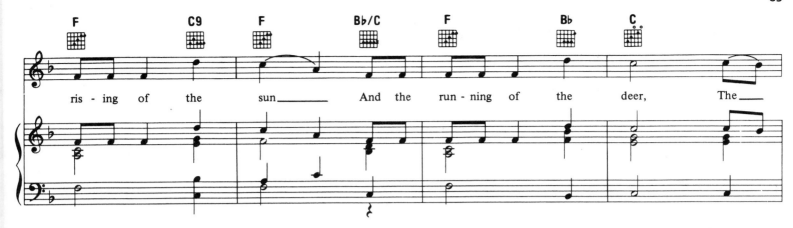

ris - ing of the sun_____ And the run - ning of the deer, The____

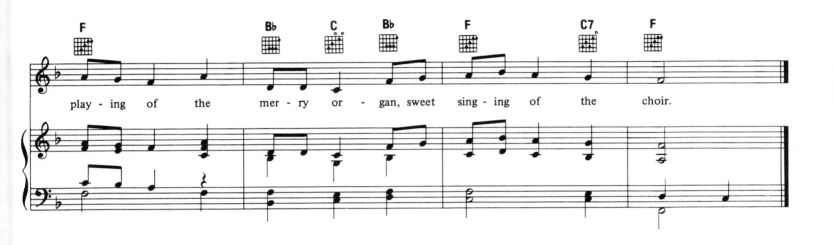

play - ing of the mer - ry or - gan, sweet sing - ing of the choir.

2. The holly bears a blossom,
As white as lily flow'r,
And Mary bore sweet Jesus Christ,
To be our sweet Saviour.

Refrain

3. The holly bears a berry,
As red as any blood,
And Mary bore sweet Jesus Christ,
To do poor sinners good.

Refrain

A HOLLY JOLLY CHRISTMAS

Music and Lyrics by
JOHNNY MARKS

(There's No Place Like)
HOME FOR THE HOLIDAYS

Words by AL STILLMAN
Music by ROBERT ALLEN

Moderato, With Feeling

HYMNE

By VANGELIS

I HEARD THE BELLS ON CHRISTMAS DAY

Words by HENRY WADSWORTH LONGFELLOW
Music by JOHN BAPTISTE CALKIN

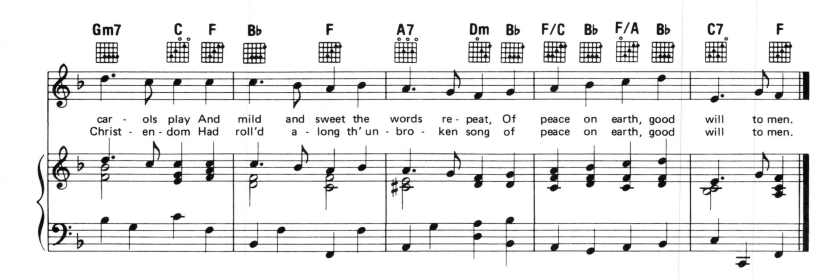

3. And in despair I bow'd my head:
   "There is no peace on earth," I said,
   "For hate is strong, and mocks the song
   Of peace on earth, good will to men."

4. Then pealed the bells more loud and deep:
   "God is not dead, nor doth He sleep;
   The wrong shall fail, the right prevail,
   With peace on earth, good will to men."

5. Till, ringing, singing on its way,
   The world revolved from night to day,
   A voice, a chime, a chant sublime,
   Of peace on earth, good will to men!

I SAW THREE SHIPS

Traditional English Carol

I HEARD THE BELLS ON CHRISTMAS DAY

Words by HENRY WADSWORTH LONGFELLOW
Adapted by JOHNNY MARKS
Music by JOHNNY MARKS

I SAW MOMMY KISSING SANTA CLAUS

Words and Music by
TOMMIE CONNOR

sleep. Then I saw Mom-my tick-le San - ta Claus,

un - der - neath his beard so snow-y white._____ Oh, what a

laugh it would have been, if Dad-dy had on - ly seen Mom-my kiss-ing San-ta Claus___

___ last night.   night.___

I'LL BE HOME FOR CHRISTMAS

Words and Music by KIM GANNON
and WALTER KENT

IT CAME UPON THE MIDNIGHT CLEAR

Words by EDMUND HAMILTON SEARS
Music by RICHARD STORRS WILLIS

I'VE GOT MY LOVE TO KEEP ME WARM

from the 20th Century Fox Motion Picture ON THE AVENUE

Words and Music by
IRVING BERLIN

The snow is snow-ing, the wind is blow-ing, but I can weath-er the storm. What do I care how much it may storm?

JESU, JOY OF MAN'S DESIRING

By JOHANN SEBASTIAN BACH

JESUS BORN ON THIS DAY

Words and Music by MARIAH CAREY
and WALTER AFANASIEFF

JINGLE-BELL ROCK

Words and Music by JOE BEAL
and JIM BOOTHE

121

JINGLE BELLS

Words and Music by
J. PIERPONT

124

JINGLE, JINGLE, JINGLE

Music and Lyrics by
JOHNNY MARKS

Moderately, Gaily

JOLLY OLD ST. NICHOLAS

Traditional 19th Century American Carol

JOY TO THE WORLD

Words by ISAAC WATTS
Music by GEORGE FRIDERIC HANDEL
Arranged by LOWELL MASON

131

THE LAST MONTH OF THE YEAR
(What Month Was Jesus Born In?)

Words and Music by VERA HALL
Adapted and Arranged by RUBY PICKENS TARTT
and ALAN LOMAX

133

MARY'S LITTLE BOY CHILD

Words and Music by
JESTER HAIRSTON

Slowly

Long time a-go in Beth-le - hem_ so the Ho - ly Bi-ble say,
Shep herds watched their flocks by night_ they saw a bright, new, shin-ing star and

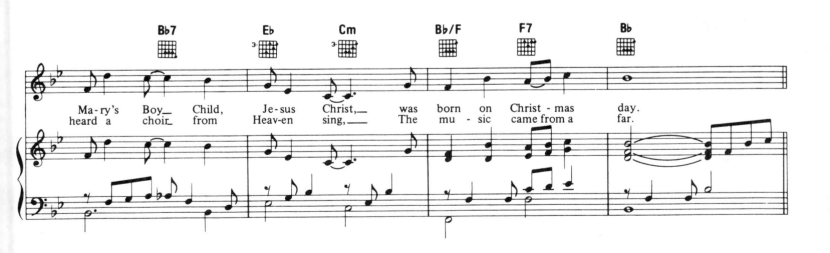

Ma-ry's Boy_ Child, Je-sus Christ,_ was born on Christ - mas day.
heard a choir_ from Heav-en sing, _ The mu - sic came from a far.

LET IT SNOW! LET IT SNOW! LET IT SNOW!

Words by SAMMY CAHN
Music by JULE STYNE

139

LITTLE SAINT NICK

Words and Music by BRIAN WILSON
and MIKE LOVE

Original key: G♭ major. This edition has been transposed up one half-step to be more playable.

LO, HOW A ROSE E'ER BLOOMING

15th Century German Carol
Translated by THEODORE BAKER
Music from *Alte Catholische Geistliche Kirchengesang*

MARCH OF THE TOYS

By VICTOR HERBERT

With Spirit

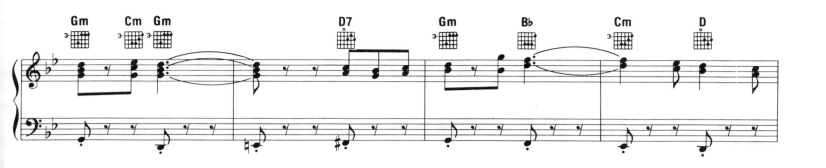

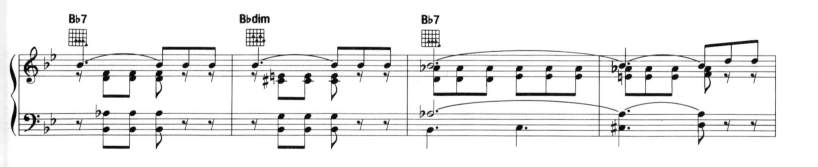

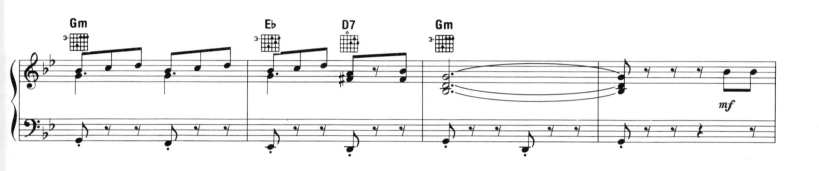

A MARSHMALLOW WORLD

Words by CARL SIGMAN
Music by PETER DE ROSE

MERRY CHRISTMAS, DARLING

Words and Music by RICHARD CARPENTER
and FRANK POOLER

154

MERRY CHRISTMAS FROM THE FAMILY

Words and Music by
ROBERT EARL KEEN

159

THE MERRY CHRISTMAS POLKA

Words by PAUL FRANCIS WEBSTER
Music by SONNY BURKE

A MERRY, MERRY CHRISTMAS TO YOU

Music and Lyrics by
JOHNNY MARKS

Very Spirited

Mer - ry Mer - ry Mer - ry Mer - ry Mer - ry

Christ - mas to you. May each day be

ver - y, ver - y hap - py all the year through.

Use any language desired.

(*) Can repeat full chorus then 4 bar vamp shouting languages, then Coda.

THE NIGHT BEFORE CHRISTMAS SONG

Music by JOHNNY MARKS
Lyrics adapted by JOHNNY MARKS
from CLEMENT MOORE'S Poem

'Twas The Night Be-fore Christ-mas and all thru the house, not a crea-ture was
up to the house-top and the rein-deer soon flew, with the sleigh full of

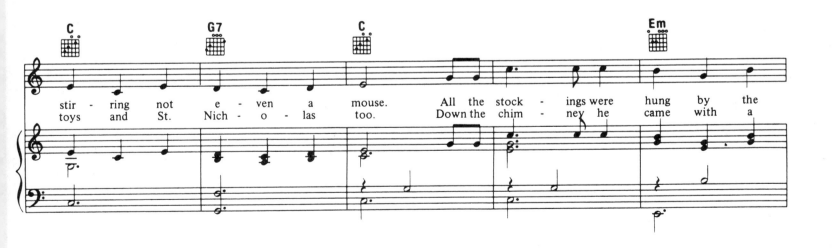

stir-ring not e-ven a mouse. All the stock-ings were hung by the
toys and St. Nich-o-las too. Down the chim-ney he came with a

THE MOST WONDERFUL DAY OF THE YEAR

Music and Lyrics by
JOHNNY MARKS

173

MY FAVORITE THINGS

from THE SOUND OF MUSIC

Lyrics by OSCAR HAMMERSTEIN II
Music by RICHARD RODGERS

NOEL! NOEL!

French-English Carol

NUTTIN' FOR CHRISTMAS

Words and Music by ROY BENNETT
and SID TEPPER

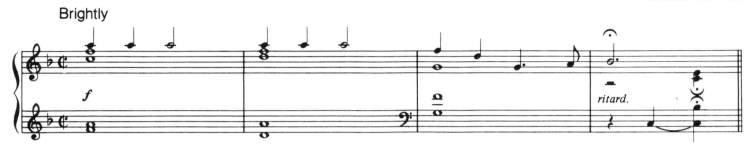

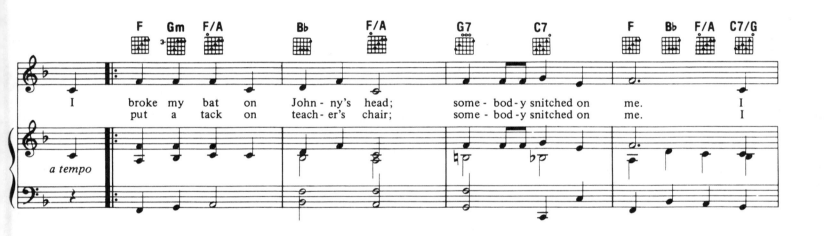

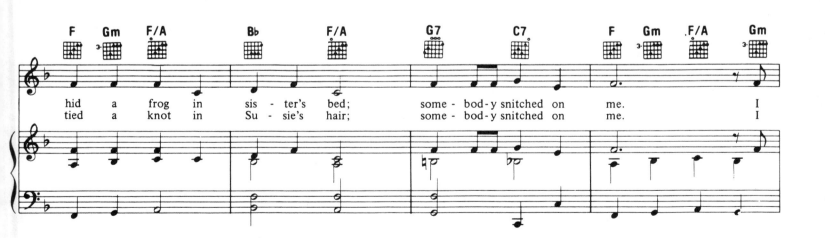

3. I won't be seeing Santa Claus; somebody snitched on me.
He won't come visit me because somebody snitched on me.
Next year I'll be going straight, next year I'll be good, just wait,
I'd start now but it's too late; somebody snitched on me. Oh,

O CHRISTMAS TREE

Traditional German Carol

Christ-mas tree! O Christ-mas tree, you stand in ver-dant beau-ty! O O
Christ-mas tree! O Christ-mas tree, much plea-sure doth thou bring me! O O
Christ-mas tree! O Christ-mas tree, thy can-dles shine out bright-ly! O O

Christ-mas tree, O Christ-mas tree, you stand in ver-dant beau-ty! Your
Christ-mas tree, O Christ-mas tree, much plea-sure doth thou bring me! For
Christ-mas tree, O Christ-mas tree, thy can-dles shine out bright-ly! Each

O COME, ALL YE FAITHFUL
(Adeste Fideles)

Words and Music by
JOHN FRANCIS WADE
Latin Words translated by FREDERICK OAKELEY

187

O COME, O COME IMMANUEL

Plainsong, 13th Century
Words translated by JOHN M. NEALE and HENRY S. COFFIN

Like an old plainsong

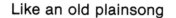

O

Guitar tacet

Come, O Come Im - man - u - el, And

ran - som cap - tive Is - ra - el, That mourns in lone - ly

heav'n - ly home. Make safe the way that leads_____ on

high And close the path to mis - er - y. Re -

joice, re - joice! Im - man - u - el shall

come to Thee, O Is - ra - el!

O LITTLE TOWN OF BETHLEHEM

Words by PHILLIPS BROOKS
Music by LEWIS H. REDNER

O HOLY NIGHT

French Words by PLACIDE CAPPEAU
English Words by JOHN S. DWIGHT
Music by ADOLPHE ADAM

O SANCTISSIMA

Sicilian Carol

Joyfully

Day of ho - li - ness, _____. peace and hap - pi - ness, _____

OLD TOY TRAINS

Words and Music by
ROGER MILLER

Old toy __ trains, __ lit-tle toy __ tracks, __ lit-tle toy __ drums __

__ com-in' from a sack, car-ried by a man dressed in white and

red. Lit-tle boy __ don't __ you think it's time you were in bed? Close your

man   dressed in white and   red.   Lit - tle boy___ don't___ you think it's time you were in

bed?   So close   your   bed?   Lit - tle boy___ don't___ you think it's time you were in

bed?

PARADE OF THE WOODEN SOLDIERS

English Lyrics by BALLARD MacDONALD
Music by LEON JESSEL

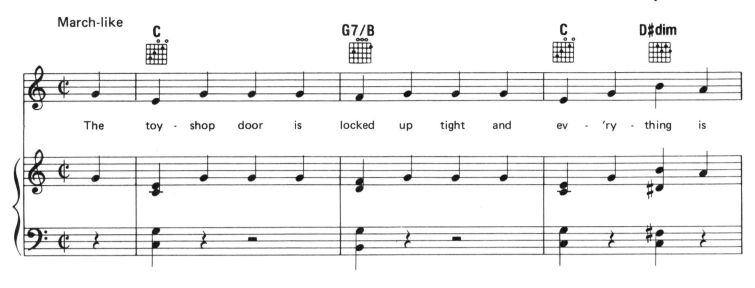

The toy - shop door is locked up tight and ev - 'ry - thing is

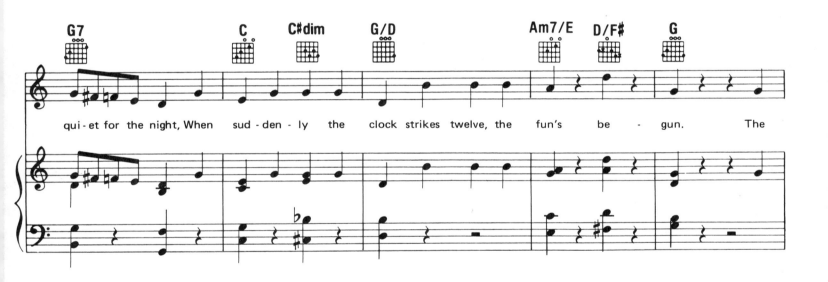

qui - et for the night, When sud - den - ly the clock strikes twelve, the fun's be - gun. The

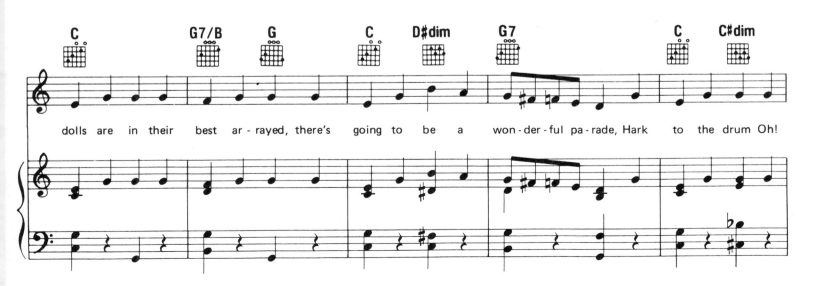

dolls are in their best ar - rayed, there's going to be a won - der - ful pa - rade, Hark to the drum Oh!

PRETTY PAPER

Words and Music by
WILLIE NELSON

ROCKIN' AROUND THE CHRISTMAS TREE

Music and Lyrics by
JOHNNY MARKS

RUDOLPH THE RED-NOSED REINDEER

Music and Lyrics by
JOHNNY MARKS

SANTA, BRING MY BABY BACK
(To Me)

Words and Music by CLAUDE DeMETRUIS
and AARON SCHROEDER

Bright rock

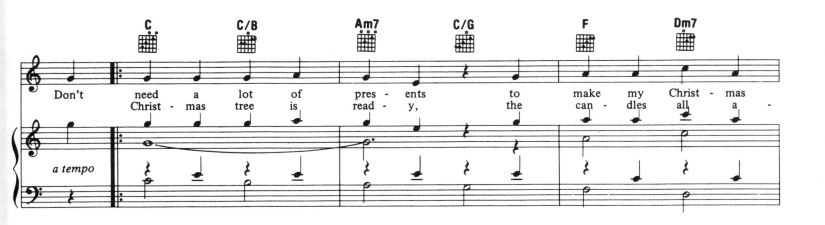

SHAKE ME I RATTLE
(Squeeze Me I Cry)

Words and Music by HAL HACKADY
and CHARLES NAYLOR

SOME CHILDREN SEE HIM

Lyric by WIHLA HUTSON
Music by ALFRED BURT

SILENT NIGHT

Words by JOSEPH MOHR
Translated by JOHN F. YOUNG
Music by FRANZ X. GRUBER

Eb   Bb   F7

Ho - ly In - fant so ten - der and mild,   Sleep   in
Heaven - ly hosts_____ sing Al - le - lu - ia,   Sleep Christ   the
With   the dawn of re - deem _____ - ing grace,   Je - sus

Bb   Bb/F

heav - en - ly peace, _____   Sleep____ in
Sav - ior is born! _____   Christ____ the
Lord   at Thy birth. _____   Je - sus

F7   1,2 Bb   3 Bb

heav - en - ly peace. _____
Sav - ior is born. _____
Lord   at Thy   birth. _____

SILVER AND GOLD

Music and Lyrics by
JOHNNY MARKS

SILVER BELLS
from the Paramount Picture THE LEMON DROP KID

Words and Music by JAY LIVINGSTON
and RAY EVANS

227

SLEEP, HOLY BABE

Words by EDWARD CASWELL
Music by J.B. DYKES

THE STAR CAROL

Lyric by WIHLA HUTSON
Music by ALFRED BURT

Tenderly with much expression

Long years a-go on a deep win-ter night,
Je-sus, the Lord was that Ba-by so small,
Dear Ba-by Je-sus, how ti-ny Thou art,

High in the heav'ns a star shone bright,
Laid down to sleep in a hum-ble stall;
I'll make a place for Thee in my heart,

While in a man-ger a wee in-fant lay,
Then came the star and it stood o-ver head,
And when the stars in the heav-ens I see,

Sweet-ly a-sleep on a bed of hay.
Shed-ding its light 'round His lit-tle bed.
Ev-er and al-ways I think of Thee.

THE TWELVE DAYS OF CHRISTMAS

Traditional English Carol

SUZY SNOWFLAKE

Words and Music by SID TEPPER
and ROY BENNETT

THAT CHRISTMAS FEELING

Words and Music by BENNIE BENJAMIN
and GEORGE WEISS

TOYLAND

Words by GLEN MacDONOUGH
Music by VICTOR HERBERT

Toy - land! Toy - land!
Child - hood's Toy - joy - land

Lit - tle girl and boy land,
Mys - tic mer - ry joy land,

239

UP ON THE HOUSETOP

Words and Music by
B.R. HANDY

WE THREE KINGS OF ORIENT ARE

Words and Music by
JOHN H. HOPKINS, JR.

Moderately

We Three Kings of O - ri - ent are;

Bear - ing gifts we tra - verse a - far,

Field and foun - tain, moor and moun - tain,

243

WE WISH YOU A MERRY CHRISTMAS

Traditional English Folksong

WHAT CHILD IS THIS?

Words by WILLIAM C. DIX
16th Century English Melody

WHEN SANTA CLAUS GETS YOUR LETTER

Music and Lyrics by
JOHNNY MARKS

WHILE SHEPHERDS WATCHED THEIR FLOCKS

Words by NAHUM TATE
Music by GEORGE FRIDERIC HANDEL

THE WHITE WORLD OF WINTER

Words by MITCHELL PARISH
Music by HOAGY CARMICHAEL

Moderately with a lift

WHO WOULD IMAGINE A KING

from the Touchstone Motion Picture THE PREACHER'S WIFE

Words and Music by MERVYN WARREN
and HALLERIN HILTON HILL

Gentle Waltz

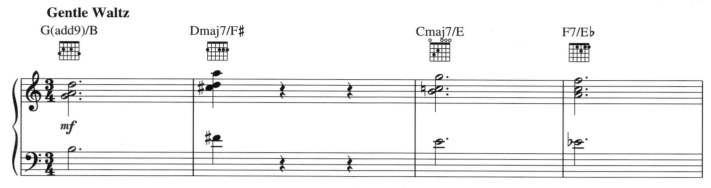

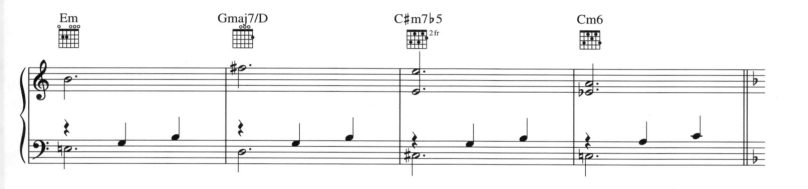

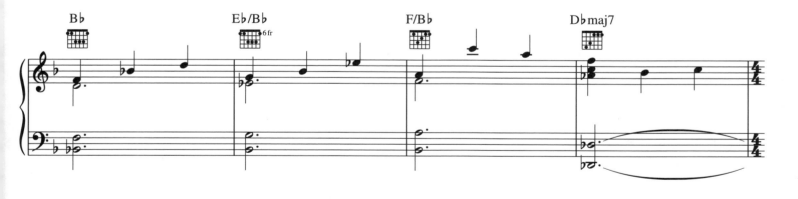

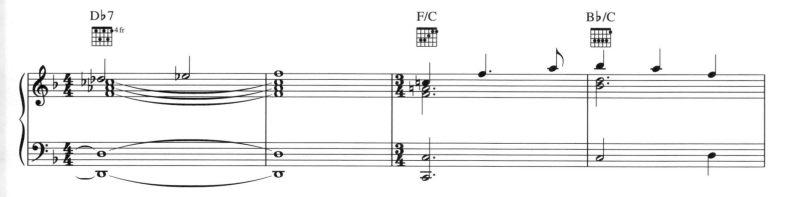

WONDERFUL CHRISTMASTIME

Words and Music by
McCARTNEY

263

THE WONDERFUL WORLD OF CHRISTMAS

Words by CHARLES TOBIAS
Music by AL FRISCH

Moderately slow

With feeling

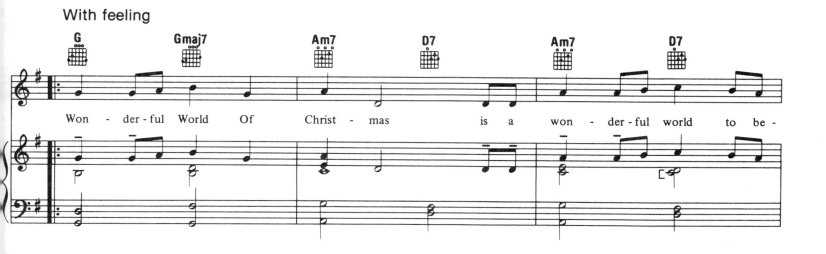

Won -der-ful World Of Christ -mas is a won -der-ful world to be- hold.

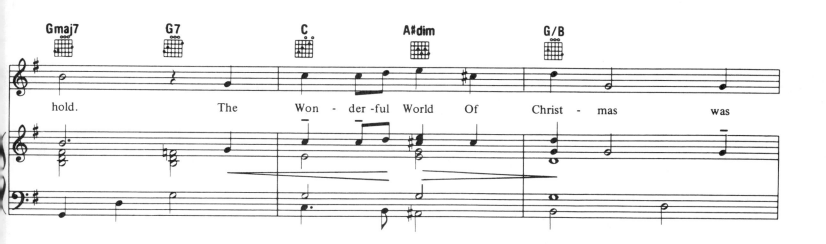

hold. The Won -der-ful World Of Christ -mas was

THE ULTIMATE SERIES

This comprehensive series features jumbo collections of piano/vocal arrangements with guitar chords. Each volume features an outstanding selection of your favorite songs. Collect them all for the ultimate music library!

Broadway Gold
100 show tunes: Beauty and the Beast • Do-Re-Mi • I Whistle a Happy Tune • The Lady Is a Tramp • Let Me Entertain You • Memory • My Funny Valentine • Oklahoma • Soon It's Gonna Rain • Some Enchanted Evening • Seventy-Six Trombones • Summer Nights • Till There Was You • Tomorrow • What I Did for Love • many more.
00361396 . . . .$21.95

Broadway Platinum
A collection of 100 popular Broadway show tunes, featuring the hits: Consider Yourself • Everything's Coming Up Roses • Getting to Know You • Gigi • Do You Hear the People Sing • I'll Be Seeing You • My Favorite Things • People • She Loves Me • Try to Remember • Younger Than Springtime • Who Can I Turn To • many more.
00311496 . . . .$19.95

Children's Songbook
66 fun songs for kids: Alphabet Song • Be Our Guest • Bingo • The Brady Bunch • Dance Little Bird (The Chicken Dance) • Do-Re-Mi • Hakuna Matata • I'm Popeye the Sailor Man • It's a Small World • Kum Ba Yah • On Top of Spaghetti • Sesame Street Theme • The Siamese Cat Song • Tomorrow • Won't You Be My Neighbor? • and more.
00310690 . . . .$17.95

Christmas – Third Edition
Includes: Angels We Have Heard on High • Carol of the Bells • Deck the Hall • The First Noel • Frosty the Snow Man • Gesu Bambino • Good King Wenceslas • Hark! the Herald Angels Sing • Here We Come A-Wassailing • Jingle-Bell Rock • Joy to the World • Nuttin' for Christmas • O Christmas Tree • O Holy Night • Rudolph the Red-Nosed Reindeer • Silent Night • What Child Is This? • and more.
00361399 . . . .$19.95

Country
Over 90 of your favorite country hits in one collection! Features: Boot Scootin' Boogie • Chattahoochie • Could I Have This Dance • Crazy • Down at the Twist And Shout • Hey, Good Lookin' • Lucille • Neon Moon • When She Cries • Where've You Been • and more.
00310036 . . . .$19.95

Gospel – 100 Songs of Devotion
Includes: El Shaddai • His Eye Is on the Sparrow • How Great Thou Art • Just a Closer Walk With Thee • Lead Me, Guide Me • (There'll Be) Peace in the Valley (For Me) • Precious Lord, Take My Hand • Wings of a Dove • more.
00241009 . . . .$19.95

Jazz Standards
Over 100 great jazz favorites, including: Ain't Misbehavin' • All of Me • Bernie's Tune • Come Rain or Come Shine • From This Moment On • Girl Talk • Here's That Rainy Day • I'll Take Romance • Imagination • Li'l Darlin' • Manhattan • Moonglow • Moonlight in Vermont • A Night in Tunisia • The Party's Over • Route 66 • Slightly Out of Tune • Solitude • Star Dust • You Turned the Tables on Me • and more.
00361407 . . . .$19.95

Latin Songs
80 hot Latin favorites, including: Amapola (Pretty Little Poppy) • Amor • Bésame Mucho (Kiss Me Much) • Blame It on the Bossa Nova • Cherry Pink and Apple Blossom White • Feelings (¿Dime?) • Frenesí • Granada • Guantanamera • Malagueña • Mambo No. 5 • Perfidia • Slightly out of Tune (Desafinado) • Tico Tico (Tico No Fuba) • What a Diff'rence a Day Made • more.
00310689 . . . .$19.95

Love and Wedding Songbook
90 songs of devotion including: The Anniversary Waltz • Canon in D • Endless Love • For All We Know • Forever and Ever, Amen • Just the Way You Are • Longer • The Lord's Prayer • Love Me Tender • One Hand, One Heart • Somewhere • Sunrise, Sunset • Through the Years • Trumpet Voluntary • and many, many more!
00361445 . . . .$19.95

FOR MORE INFORMATION, SEE YOUR LOCAL MUSIC DEALER, OR WRITE TO:

HAL•LEONARD® CORPORATION
7777 W. BLUEMOUND RD. P.O. BOX 13819 MILWAUKEE, WI 53213

http://www.halleonard.com

Prices, contents, and availability subject to change without notice. Availability and pricing may vary outside the U.S.A.

Movie Music
Over 70 favorites from the big screen, including: Also Sprach Zarathustra • Can You Feel the Love Tonight • Chariots of Fire • Cinema Paridiso • Cruella De Vil • Driving Miss Daisy • Easter Parade • Forrest Gump • Moon River • That Thing You Do! • Viva Las Vegas • The Way We Were • When I Fall in Love • and more.
00310240 . . . .$17.95

Rock 'N' Roll
100 classics, including: All Shook Up • Bye Bye Love • Chantilly Lace • Duke of Earl • Gloria • Hello Mary Lou • I Only Want to Be With You • It's My Party • Johnny B. Goode • The Loco-Motion • Lollipop • Rock Around the Clock • Surfin' U.S.A. • A Teenager in Love • The Twist • Wooly Bully • Yakety Yak • and more.
00361411 . . . .$21.95

Singalong!
100 of the best-loved popular songs ever: Ain't Misbehavin' • All of Me • Beer Barrel Polka • California, Here I Come • The Candy Man • Crying in the Chapel • Edelweiss • Feelings • Five Foot Two, Eyes of Blue • For Me and My Gal • Goodnight Irene • I Left My Heart in San Francisco • Indiana • It's a Small World • Que Sera, Sera • This Land Is Your Land • Too Fat Polka • When Irish Eyes Are Smiling • and more.
00361418 . . . .$17.95

Standard Ballads
100 mellow masterpieces, including: Angel Eyes • Body and Soul • Darn That Dream • Day By Day • Easy to Love • In The Still of the Night • Isn't It Romantic? • Misty • Mona Lisa • Moon River • My Funny Valentine • Smoke Gets in Your Eyes • When I Fall in Love • and more.
00310246 . . . .$19.95

Swing Standards
Over 90 songs to get you swinging, including: Bandstand Boogie • Boogie Woogie Bugle Boy • Cherokee • Don't Get Around Much Anymore • Heart and Soul • How High the Moon • In the Mood • Moonglow • Satin Doll • Sentimental Journey • Witchcraft • and more.
00310245 . . . .$19.95

0701

Christmas Collections
From Hal Leonard
All books arranged for piano, voice, & guitar.

And The Angels Sing
A beautiful collection of 22 classic Christmas carols – some dating back to the 14th century – and full-color reproductions of medieval and renaissance paintings from the Museum of Fine Arts in Boston. Songs include: Silent Night, Holy Night • O Holy Night • Ave Maria • The First Noel • and more.
00311531 ....$15.95

The Best Christmas Songs Ever
A collection of more than 60 of the best-loved songs of the season, including: Blue Christmas • Frosty The Snow Man • Grandma Got Run Over by a Reindeer • I'll Be Home For Christmas • Jingle-Bell Rock • Rudolph, The Red-Nosed Reindeer • Silver Bells • You're All I Want for Christmas • and many more.
00359130 ....$18.95

The Big Book Of Christmas Songs
An outstanding collection of over 120 all-time Christmas favorites and hard-to-find classics. Features: Angels We Have Heard On High • As Each Happy Christmas • Auld Lang Syne • The Boar's Head Carol • Christ Was Born On Christmas Day • Bring A Torch Jeanette, Isabella • Carol Of The Bells • Coventry Carol • Deck The Halls • The First Noel • The Friendly Beasts • God Rest Ye Merry Gentlemen • I Heard The Bells On Christmas Day • It Came Upon A Midnight Clear • Jesu, Joy Of Man's Desiring • Joy To The World • Masters In This Hall • O Holy Night • The Story Of The Shepherd • 'Twas The Night Before Christmas • What Child Is This? • and many more. Includes guitar chord frames.
00311520 ....$19.95

Season's Greetings
A great big collection of 50 favorites, including: All I Want for Christmas Is You • Blue Christmas • The Christmas Song • Frosty the Snow Man • Grandma Got Run Over by a Reindeer • Happy Holiday • I'll Be Home for Christmas • Most of All I Wish You Were Here • Silver Bells • What Made the Baby Cry? • and more.
00310426 ....$16.95

Christmas Songs For Kids
27 songs kids love to play during the holidays, including: Away In A Manger • The Chipmunk Song • Deck The Hall • The First Noel • Jingle Bells • Joy To The World • O Christmas Tree • Silent Night • and more.
00311571 ....$7.95

Contemporary Christian Christmas
20 songs as recorded by today's top Christian artists, including: Michael W. Smith (All Is Well) • Sandi Patty (Bethlehem Morning) • Amy Grant (Breath of Heaven) • Michael Card (Celebrate the Child) • Steven Curtis Chapman (Going Home for Christmas) • Michael English (Mary Did You Know?) • Steve Green (Rose of Bethlehem) • 4Him (A Strange Way to Save the World) • Point of Grace (This Gift) • Scott Wesley Brown (This Little Child) • and more.
00310643 ....$12.95

The Definitive Christmas Collection
All the Christmas songs you need in one convenient collection! Over 110 classics in all! Songs include: An Old Fashioned Christmas • Away In A Manger • Blue Christmas • The Chipmunk Song • Christmas Is • The Christmas Waltz • Do They Know It's Christmas • Feliz Navidad • The First Noel • Frosty The Snow Man • The Greatest Gift Of All • Happy Holiday • A Holly Jolly Christmas • I Saw Mommy Kissing Santa Claus • Jingle-Bell Rock • Mister Santa • My Favorite Things • O Holy Night • Rudolph, The Red-Nosed Reindeer • Santa, Bring My Baby Back (To Me) • Silent Night • Suzy Snowflake • We Need A Little Christmas • You're All I Want For Christmas • and many more.
00311602 ....$29.95

The Lighter Side of Christmas
42 fun festive favorites, including: Grandma Got Run Over by a Reindeer • A Holly Jolly Christmas • I Guess There Ain't No Santa Claus • I Saw Mommy Kissing Santa Claus • Jingle-Bell Rock • The Merry Christmas Polka • Rockin' Around the Christmas Tree • Rudolph the Red-Nosed Reindeer • That's What I'd Like for Christmas • and more.
00310628 ....$14.95

Ultimate Christmas
100 seasonal favorites, including: All Through the Night • Auld Lang Syne • Blue Christmas • Bring a Torch, Jeanette, Isabella • Carol of the Bells • The Chipmunk Song • The First Noel • Frosty the Snow Man • Gesu Bambino • Goin' on a Sleighride • Happy Holiday • Happy Xmas (War Is Over) • Hymne • Jesu, Joy of Man's Desiring • Jingle-Bell Rock • March of the Toys • My Favorite Things • The Night Before Christmas Song • Pretty Paper • Silver and Gold • Silver Bells • Sleigh Ride • Suzy Snowflake • What Child Is This • The Wonderful World of Christmas • and more.
00361399 ....$19.95

FOR MORE INFORMATION, SEE YOUR LOCAL MUSIC DEALER, OR WRITE TO:

HAL•LEONARD®
CORPORATION
7777 W. BLUEMOUND RD. P.O. BOX 13819 MILWAUKEE, WI 53213
http://www.halleonard.com
PRICES, CONTENTS, AND AVAILABILITY SUBJECT TO CHANGE WITHOUT NOTICE.

0601